THE ULTIMATE ROBLOX HANDBOOK

Printed exclusively for Baker and Taylor

First published in Great Britain in 2020 by Mortimer Children's Books
An imprint of Welbeck Children's Limited, part of the Welbeck
Publishing Group, 20 Mortimer Street, London W1T 3JW

This edition published in the United States in 2021 by
Mortimer Children's Books
An imprint of Welbeck Children's Limited, part of the
Welbeck Publishing Group

ISBN: 978 1 83935 106 8

Printed in Dongguan, China

10 9 8 7 6 5 4 3 2 1

Designed and packaged by: Dynamo Limited
Writer: Kevin Pettman
Design Manager: Matt Drew
Editorial Manager: Joff Brown
Production: Freencky Portas

MORTIMER

THE ULTIMATE ROBLOX HANDBOOK

MORTIMER

CONTENTS

WHAT'S INSIDE

ROBLOX RULES! IT'S AN ACTION-PACKED, ADVENTUROUS AND CREATIVE GAME ENJOYED BY MILLIONS.

Unique universes, special places and cool characters combine to complete tasks, join leaderboards and have a laugh with friends. You can even design and build your own games!

This expert ROBLOX guidebook will raise your gaming skills and knowledge to the next level. It's time to check out epic tips, info, secrets and facts to make you a block-busting pro and get ahead of the rest. Enjoy this ROBLOX ride to becoming a master player!

CONTENTS

PRO PLAYER POWER

ROBLOX ROUND-UP
TOP TIPS FOR PROS TO KNOW!

1

> FRIENDLY FORCE

Pro ROBLOX players learn from, share with and talk to their online friends and community. Discuss game tips, secrets and strategies and if you create something sick, tell your screen pals!

2

> TAKE CONTROL

To boost control and accuracy with things like mouse settings, keyboard and Xbox controllers, top gamers adjust these through **in-game settings** and sensitivity. Alter graphics mode and quality for optimum performance.

3

> PRACTICE PLAY

ROBLOX experts are very familiar with the homepage, along with what the **Games**, **Catalog**, **Create** and **Robux** tabs do. Spend time learning these functions and explore options on the left of the screen, such as **Profile**, **Avatar** and **Inventory**.

4

> ROCKIN' ROBUX

Having Robux (in-game cash) gives you the bonus of cosmetic avatar upgrades, If you pay real money to join the **Builders Club**, you'll have Robux dished out daily!

BUILDERS CLUB BADGES

> BRILLIANT BUILDS

Enter the world of **ROBLOX Studio** to put your building knowledge to the test! Here, elite gamers create games and builds for the community. It takes time to master, but it's well worth it.

> ENTER EVENTS

Towards the bottom left on the home page is **Events**. These themed games could be based on holidays, movies or fun features – enter them and become a better player!

> DEVELOPER DETAILS

The best players know who the best ROBLOX developers are. People like Alexnewtron (MeepCity), Dued1 (Work at a Pizza Place) and callmehbob (Royale High) have created ROBLOX's biggest games. Check out the cool stuff they do and say!

ALEX NEWTRON

DUED1'S WORK AT A PIZZA PLACE

SCREEN & CONTROLS

GET TO GRIPS WITH WHAT YOU SEE AND CONTROL WITH THIS QUICK-FIRE GUIDE FOR ELITE USERS!

CAMERA ANGLES

If the game you're playing doesn't need to be fixed to a preset camera, you can toggle between in-game camera modes. Just make sure **Shift Lock Switch** is turned on in **Settings**. Classic (fixed) or Follow (rotating) camera views can be selected around your avatar.

DYNAMIC - - - - -> VIEWS

<- - - - - CHECK IT OUT IN VR!

VIRTUAL REALITY

Users can enjoy a virtual reality (VR) experience with ROBLOX! VR is when a gamer wears a special headset mask to create a 3D-gaming environment. VR is supported across PC, Mac and Xbox. In **Settings**, VR Mode must be on and through **Menu**, the **VR Radial Menu** shows a list of super cool options.

CHAT BACK

Xbox players have the option to use the voice chat system, depending on your settings and if you have a headset. If you have an Xbox Live subscription, **Party Chat** lets you chat to your Xbox Live friends. Switch to normal in-game chat through the **Your Party** and **Switch to Game Chat** settings.

AVATAR SKILLS - - - - →

GAME ON

Keep an eye on factors like popularity, ratings and the **About** description to help you choose the best games and save time.

MEGA MOVES

The ROBLOX Animation Series lets your character bust out dance moves and motions. In the in-game chat option, type instructions like **/e laugh** and **/e dance** and **/e cheer** to see these wacky actions. In the Work at a Pizza Place game, there are even special emoji dance buttons to click like **HipHop**, **Flair** and **Shuffle**!

★

EXPERT BONUS!

During a game, PC and Mac players can click the **Menu** button (top left), then **Help** to display keyboard and mouse control options.

XBOX EXTRA

Since 2015, ROBLOX has been available on Xbox One. Gamers can remind themselves of the Xbox controls by clicking the little **Menu** button on the controller. You'll see things like toggle, tool, nav, move, jump and camera rotation.

ADVANCED AVATAR

ALL YOU NEED TO KNOW ABOUT CREATING AND CONTROLLING YOUR ROBLOX CHARACTER!

ORIGINAL BASIC AVATAR

R6 MODE

From the homepage, the Avatar Editor tool is the place to alter and design your character. It has tabs to play with areas like **Clothing**, **Animations** and **Body**. Pro ROBLOX users will know that the current most basic mode is called 'R6'. These have just six body parts and look very blocky.

R6 R15

3D

Avatar is the official ROBLOX word for the character you design and play games through. You are the avatar and the avatar is you – pretty much! You can make your avatar look just like you, or look totally different. Maybe your avatar is a cool, super hero, daredevil version of you!

R15 AND RTHRO EXPLAINED

'R15' mode arrived in 2016, offering the choice of a more flexible avatar with 15 joints and firmer articulation and movements.

EXPERT BONUS!
If you hear a pro player call an avatar a Robloxian, don't be confused – the two words mean the same thing!

R6   R15

3D

Body Type   0%

CHECK OUT THE LONGER LEGS AND SLIMMED-DOWN LOOK!

R6   R15

3D

Body Type   100%

Players can edit and scale their avatar to select the perfect proportions. In **Editor**, select **Body**, then **Appearance** and **Scale**. **Height**, **Width**, **Head** and **Proportions** can all be changed on a percentage scale. A **Body Type** set to 0% produces an avatar with true R15 proportions. Change this to 100% to adopt the new Rthro proportions.

The release of 'Rthro' proportions in 2018 caused a shockwave in the ROBLOX fandom – some users loved it, others said it looked too realistic for the game!

AVATAR: GET THE LOOK

TO HELP YOU LOCK DOWN THE FRESHEST LOOKS AND COSTUME CREATIONS, CHECK OUT THESE OUTFIT TYPES AND TIPS...

So, ROBLOX avatars can have a basic R6, advanced R15 or super-advanced Rthro look and proportions. Luckily, ROBLOX says it will always keep the original 'blocky' avatar options of R6 and R15 and make costumes available across all three. The technical term for this is 'backward compatibility'.

⭐ EXPERT BONUS!

Another top tip is to click on your avatar image in **Editor**, then drag it around to see what it looks like from every camera angle!

> STREET SMART

Stick the Red Roblox Cap, Orange Shades, Jean Shorts or Bricky shorts on your avatar to become a **sick street-smart dude**! This gear can all be picked up for **free**. If you do have spare Robux, why not splash out a little on some Adidas joggers or a shirt to look like an elite street character!

TRY ON SOME HEROIC GEAR!

< CLEVER KID

Never underestimate the power of a classic nerd or '**Geek Sheek**' avatar look! Gamers could mistake you for a kindly soul, just before you steql in on a game win, or take a bonus leaderboard position. Ha! Team a pair of glasses with a retro t-shirt and the job is done.

SMART STUFF

> BOSSIN' IT

In ROBLOX tycoon games, you might want an avatar look that shows you **mean business** and you're ready to make money! Try searching for a 'Manager' look, or create your own with a white shirt, tie and formal pants (trousers). Gamers will take you seriously as you coin in some **serious cash**, too!

< SUPER HERO

There are loads of cool ways to get a super hero design into your avatar. For example, keep an eye on any **official skins** ROBLOX releases around Marvel films. We love the Ant Man mask from 2018! A super hero outfit will make the rest of the ROBLOX world stand back and respect you.

GIVE 'EM A FRIGHT

> SCARY SIGHT

Want to put the frighteners on the rest of the ROBLOX world? Dress up in scary gear and make the others run a mile! Obviously it's all **just for fun** and you're a nice character underneath it, but red or black outfits and a menacing face will get this look locked down.

AWESOME AVATARS!

GOING SHOPPING FOR EPIC GEAR AND ITEMS FOR YOUR AVATAR? CHECK OUT THIS ADVICE FIRST!

On the ROBLOX homepage, the Catalog tab is where you can change and update the look and dress of your character. Remember that these are just cosmetic things and they don't boost your character's in-game powers! Looking fab does help you to stand out from the ROBLOX crowd though.

CHANGING ROOMS

With hundreds of options in the **Catalog** shop, choosing how to spend your Robux can take a while. Hit the try on button for a quick preview of what you'll look like with a particular shirt, head or accessory. Try before you buy and don't waste your cash!

I'LL TAKE IT!

Try On

GRAB A FREEBIE!

If you don't have any Robux you can still create a **fresh feel** for your avatar. In the drop down menu, sort the items in price order from **low to high** to see all the stuff that **doesn't cost a penny**. Pick what you want for free and show it off to your online friends.

Relevance

Most Favorited

Bestselling

Recently Updated

BARGAIN!

Price (High to Low)

Price (Low to High)

VINTAGE STYLE

Click on your profile, on the left side of the home page, to view any collections that you have saved. You can switch between things you've selected in the past and even return to a look and outfit you had **forgotten all about**.

GET YOURSELF A THEME

Genre filters are a speedy and clever way to search for a particular avatar style. You can tick boxes such as **Sports**, **Comedy**, **Sc-Fi** and **Fighting**. For example, if it's Halloween and you want a scary outfit, click the **Horror** option and ghostly gear will appear!

Building

✓ Horror

Town and City

Comedy

SPOOKY

PRO PLAYER POWER

TOP TECH TALK

DO SOME PRO-LEVEL ROBLOX WORDS AND PHRASES CONFUSE YOU? THEN FLICK THROUGH THIS JARGON-BUSTING GUIDE!

DEVEX

Also known as Developer Exchange, this is a scheme that lets top developers turn their Robux into **real money**. This will have been earned through selling things like passes, items and VIP servers.

GUI

Pros often use the term graphical user interface, or GUI for short. It refers to the information and navigation elements on the screen. Think of it as the **link** between the gamer and the computer.

⭐ EXPERT BONUS!

More ROBLOX words and phrases are explained in the glossary on page 62.

TERRAIN

Terrain means the landscape or environment in a game. Creators talk about this a lot, including smooth and flat terrain types.

NPC

Watch out for a NPC! Non-playable characters can appear in lots of game types, from Town & City to Tycoon and Survival. They are the characters **not controlled by other ROBLOX players**.

SPAMMING

In ROBLOX, spamming is a word that means a gamer is saying or doing the same thing **again and again**. Spamming can be very annoying to others in the game!

TOTALLY GANGSTER!

WASD

The **WASD** keys are vital for PC and Mac users! It's a well-known gaming term and means the **W** (forward), **A** (left), **S** (back) and **D** (right) keys on a keyboard and the functions and controls they perform.

VIRTUAL REALITY

In the virtual reality (VR) system, ROBLOX uses the Oculus Rift and HTC Vive headset gear. These are two of the coolest bits of VR gaming gear you can get your hands on!

COOLEST DUDE IN ROBLOXIA?

ROBLOXIA

You may have heard of Robloxia, but what is it? Robloxia is a useful and wide-ranging phrase that can describe a city, street, map location and even the whole ROBLOX universe. Wow!

I PLAY SAFE & STAY SAFE

THE ROBLOX WORLD IS FUN AND ADVENTUROUS AND IT'S GREAT TO SHARE IT WITH FRIENDS, BUT STAYING SAFE ONLINE IS VITAL.

> PARENTAL SET-UP

If you're new to ROBLOX, always download the game and set up your avatar with a parent or guardian. Together you can work through any **technical issues** you may have and register your account safely and correctly. It is important for adults to know what the game is about.

Parents can set up controls, such as making an account so that it can only communicate with gamers they've already accepted as friends. There is also a setting so that a player cannot accept friend requests.

> CHAT CONTROLS

Chat is the system that allows players to communicate with others in a game through typing text or voice chat. This can be programmed to allow chat, restrict chat (to just with a player's accepted friends) or no chat.

> GAME CHOICE

Account Restrictions can be added for gamers under 13. This will mean that they can only access and play from a list of games appropriate for their age. **Account Restrictions** is located through the **Settings** menu.

> FILTER FORCE

Language filters are in operation on ROBLOX. These are designed to help **stop bad words** appearing in games. There are also filters that pre-review images, video and sound files before they appear on the site. A ROBLOX moderation team is always online too.

> REPORTING & BLOCKING

If a player does something against the ROBLOX Community Rules and is behaving poorly, they can be reported and blocked. A player can be blocked by clicking on their profile page, or in-game by selecting them from the leaderboard and choosing **block player** or **report player** from the menu options.

> PERSONAL DETAILS

Never reveal your first name, surname, address, email, phone number or school name online. Your avatar username should not include any of these. **Never** click on a link that promises free Robux as ROBLOX does not offer this.

IMPORTANT!

Enter your true date of birth when setting up your ROBLOX account. This decides if you are placed in the under 13 or over 13 years old category. A player's age is shown on the home page, in the top right next to their name. The '13+' symbol means that they are 13 or older, and <13 shows that they are 12 or younger.

LET THE GAMES BEGIN

THERE ARE THOUSANDS OF AWESOME ROBLOX GAMES TO CHOOSE FROM.

Whether you're a fan of Survival, Tycoon, Building, Town and City, Role Play, Superhero or many other game genres, get ready for the greatest guide to help make you a pro player!

EXPERT APPEAL

☑ Expert advice

☑ Top tips

☑ Secrets & stats

☑ Fun facts

ROLE-PLAYING GAMES

ALSO KNOWN AS RPGS, THESE MAKE UP SOME OF THE MOST POPULAR AND LEGENDARY GAMES EVER TO HIT ROBLOX!

A typical RPG will see your avatar enter a situation, event or scene and have to complete tasks and missions. Often this is to get rewards, including money or leaderboard points. A Role-Playing Game can have crossovers with other genres, like Town and City or Tycoon.

RPGs can have fantastic scenery and landscapes, and are often not as confined as First Person Shooters or Tycoon games. Be aware that most of the rewards and items to find will be in **obvious places**. For example, it's highly unlikely that a developer will place a cool vehicle to use in the middle of nowhere!

RPGs can demand **a lot of time and practice**. They are not the easiest to quickly dip in and out of. To become a top RPG user, you've got to put the hours in! It's good to have a structure and game strategy at the start, but the best players react to situations and have the **confidence to adapt** to in-game developments. Be brave and bold!

EXPERT BONUS!

Use the third-person camera view in Jailbreak to get a great view of exactly what's around your avatar.

OBLOXIAN HIGHSCHOOL

SCHOOL'S OUT!

Keep an eye on the **leaderboard**, on the top right, as you'll want to keep pace with the best players in the server. Use any top-down map views that RPGs have on screen. This will show you the area you're in and any hazards nearby, plus any interesting zones to head towards.

RPG: EXPERT APPEAL

- ☑ Packed with adventure
- ☑ Huge environments to explore
- ☑ Find, collect, complete missions
- ☑ Often danger elements

JAILBREAK

Is this legendary game, with 2.7 billion visits, classed as RPG? It definitely is, as well as being in the Town and City genre. Be a crim-chasing cop or a cop-dodging crim, and do your stuff! As a top-level officer, use the **most wanted** display board to hunt big-bounty baddies. Tips for criminals include hunting a keycard for escapes and bank robberies, and upgrading cars for speedy escapes. Bad guys can work as a team, too!

STATS

👍 **VISITS** 2.7 billion

🔧 **DATE CREATED** January 2017

👤 **CREATED BY** Badimo

✚ **MAX PLAYERS** 26

ROCITIZENS

RPGs can be laidback and a bit whacky. RoCitizens has had 400+ million visits because it's exactly that! You'll get a job like law enforcement, medic, food clerk or cashier. You'll **pocket base pay and task bonuses** for the missions you complete. It's then time to create a home, explore the town and mix with others. To bank the cash, complete quests accurately and don't leave as your shift will mean nothing!

STATS

- 👍 **VISITS** 405 million
- 🔧 **DATE CREATED** December 2013
- 👤 **CREATED BY** Firebrand1
- ➕ **MAX PLAYERS** 20

SWORDBURST 2

This action game goes under the radar with less than 100 million views, but ROBLOX users know it's a **smash**! Teleport between worlds, see off enemies, pick up gear and battle the bosses. The key to SB2 is levelling up for greater armour. Attack mobs on each floor, like crabs, boars and knights, to **gather experience**. Skilled fighters are ready for defeated mobs to lose their weapons – these are called drops.

STATS

👍 **VISITS** 76 million
🔧 **DATE CREATED** February 2017
👤 **CREATED BY** Swordburst 2
🧍 **MAX PLAYERS** 15

Become one of the famous Animatronic World characters, such as a cat, squirrel, bear or rabbit. Then **jump into this sandbox universe** for hours of fun. AW has a huge social world, and interacting with users is a big part of this RPG. Make sure you work with your friends to hunt reward badges – even silly things like clicking on the Redfur NPC's nose can deliver you one!

STATS

👍 **VISITS** 90 million
🔧 **DATE CREATED** April 2014
👤 **CREATED BY** Gommy_Renard
🧍 **MAX PLAYERS** 30

EXPERT GAME GUIDE

TOWN AND CITY

FROM MEEPCITY TO WORK AT A PIZZA PLACE, ROBLOXIAN HIGH SCHOOL AND MAD CITY DOGS, TOWN AND CITY COVERS A MEGA VARIETY OF QUALITY GAMES!

As the genre name suggests, Town and City feature built-up environments with lots of players in the server, NPCs, vehicles and big structures over many terrains. Be ready for something unusual to happen in these games!

Try to quickly discover which jobs pay the best cash. That way you'll bank more, and be able to upgrade equipment and reach new levels at a faster rate. Of course gaming is about having **bags of fun**, but if you can gain bags of cash as well, you'll have an even better time! Be sure to keep clear of nasty NPCs, though.

They can be for single players, teams or users briefly working together to achieve an aim. Even when expert players first started out as newbies, they **took the time to watch** what others do in Town and City games and learn from them. Use the chat feature and ask others questions to improve your knowledge!

TOWN AND CITY: EXPERT APPEAL

- ✔ Never-ending environments
- ✔ Huge social interaction
- ✔ Combine adventure and building
- ✔ Suits long or short game time

MAD CITY

The aim of ROBLOX games is usually to be the best and reach the highest scores and levels. In Town and City, it doesn't hurt to be a **little flashy** and to **show off**! Creating the best house on the street and blingin' up the coolest car will be impressive and show the gaming community that you're a pro not to be messed with!

EXPERT BONUS!

Town and City are the perfect games to sharpen your all-round skills – it can mix Roleplay, Action, Tycoon, Building and First Person Shooter.

GOOD DOG!

WORK AT A PIZZA PLACE

Take a job, work hard, cooperate with the team and you can earn plenty of 'moneyz' in this **billion-busting game**. The manager's position is the most prized and difficult to take – even though you can pay 80 Robux to teleport into the post as soon as it's free. But the manager doesn't earn more, so instead, focus on the daily Double Time bonus to **rake in big bucks**!

STATS

👍 **VISITS** 1.6 billion

🔧 **DATE CREATED** March 2008

👤 **CREATED BY** Dued1

👥 **MAX PLAYERS** 12

MAD CITY

Mad City is a bit like a ROBLOX franchise – there's Mad City Airport and Mad City Prison Break – but the **canine connection** is by far the best! Choose to be a police officer and **adopt and customize a police dog** to take down the bad dudes! You'll need the Pet Plus pass (100 Robux) and this means the dog will follow you around the map and attack crims for you to handcuff. Best Mad City update ever!

STATS

👍 **VISITS** 427.7 million

🔧 **DATE CREATED** December 2017

👤 **CREATED BY** Schwifty Studios

👥 **MAX PLAYERS** 26

MEEPCITY

The first ROBLOX game to smash one billion visits and with well over two billion by 2019, MeepCity is an **iconic place** for game fans. Bursting with action and adventure, your avatar can take part in mini games, go fishing, build and furnish a house, turn up at parties and interact with others on the server.

You can buddy up in MeepCity by buying your own pet, called a Meep. You can choose its colour and even name it! Head to the Pet Shop to pick up a Meep for 100 coins. Customizing options range from new hairstyles to headgear, which are good value at under 100 coins, to hats that cost thousands. Experienced 'Meepers' **don't waste cash** on mega-expensive Meep items!

FISHING FOR CASH

One of the main ways to generate coins is to go fishing. Charge up your fishing rod and **aim for dark spots** in the water where the fish lurk. Different fish can then be sold for coins in the Pet Shop. Remember you can only have 20 fish in your bucket.

EXPERT BONUS!

Hugely popular games like MeepCity are often called MMORPG titles. This stands for massively multiplayer online role-playing game.

GET INTO GEAR

Master Meepers will always **upgrade their fishing rod** by spending coins. The better your rod, the better chance you have of catching valuable rare fish. **Save up** for the gold rod (1,500 coins) for a higher chance of fishing out a prized catch!

STATS		
👍	**VISITS** 3.7 billion	
🔧	**DATE CREATED** February 2016	
👤	**CREATED BY** alexnewtron	
🧱	**MAX PLAYERS** 130	

TYCOON GAMES

BOOST YOUR CASH-CRAZY SKILLS BY JUMPING INTO THE WORLD OF ROBLOX TYCOON GAMES!

You need to make money and also stand out from the crowd by building your own amazing games and attractions in these games. Restaurant Tycoon, Lumber Tycoon and Retail Tycoon are great starting places. The key is to start small and build your empire up slowly. You'll always need a steady stream of income.

★ EXPERT BONUS!

Not all Tycoon games have 'Tycoon' in the title. Look for the genre listing in the game description and read the details to make sure you don't miss a cool new Tycoon release.

DESIGN A RESTAURANT

In Retail Tycoon, begin with the cheaper register (checkout) and shelving items to help raise your first funds. **Don't waste time** by saving up for flashier items – get the bucks rolling in asap!

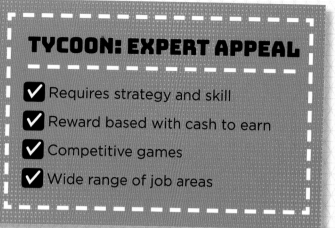

Keeping an eye on your stock levels, whether it's food or general store items, is **crucial.** An expert Tycoon manager knows what the funds are in their account and keeps their stores well stocked to keep the customers coming in. 'Footfall' is the **technical term** for how busy your shop is.

Don't be afraid to start again because not every business will be a success at first. If you have very few customers and cash is limited, cut your losses, **quit the game and begin again.** Always check out what the competition is doing to pick up money-making tips.

THEME PARK TYCOON 2

THEME PARK TYCOON 2 IS THE PERFECT TYCOON GAME TO TEST YOUR MONEY-BUILDING POWERS.

You can build, create and work out your own rules for raking in the cash – plus have a laugh on the rides at the same time! A trip to a theme park during school holidays can be the most epic thing – now you can build your own rockin' ROBLOX rides! Take the quick tutorial if you need help on basic buttons and functions.

★ EXPERT BONUS!

Add trash cans to your park, which can be found in the **paths** button. Otherwise you'll be picking up all of the rubbish yourself!

The aim in Theme Park Tycoon is to get people to pay to enter your park and **splash cash** for rides. Then you'll earn more money to pay for more brilliant buildings!

BUILD IT ON UP

You're able to explore other users' parks, but you'll need to **master the building process** to construct fun rides and attractions. Using the picker tool, click something that's already on your land to repeat the build quickly.

CUSTOMER FEEDBACK

Keep an eye on the 'thoughts' and 'stats' of your rides, stalls and attractions. It reveals what your visitors think and the **ways you can improve** the park. You can also see how long rides last for and if you need to make them longer or shorter to get more paying guests.

⭐ EXPERT BONUS!

Once you've built an exciting park with a mix of fun rollercoasters, water and train rides that people queue to use, try increasing the entrance price. That way your money will get a big boost. Don't make it too costly though because you'll turn vital visitors away!

BAD INVESTMENT

When picking a gentle ride to build, choose the observation tower and **not the spiral slide**. It costs $2900, which is $1300 more than the spiral, but can take 11 guests at the same time. The slide lets only one user on each time, which is not good for your bank balance!

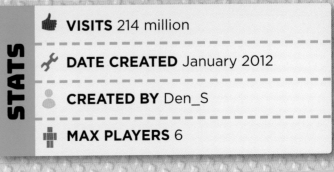

STATS

👍 **VISITS** 214 million

🔧 **DATE CREATED** January 2012

👤 **CREATED BY** Den_S

🔢 **MAX PLAYERS** 6

SIMULATOR GAMES

DITCH THE REAL WORLD TO BECOME A HERO IN AN EPIC VARIETY OF SITUATIONS. FROM FLYING TO MINING, SUPER HEROES TO DINOSAURS, AND BATTLES WITH GAMERS AND NPCS!

Games like Jailbreak, Work at a Pizza Place, Phantom Forces and even Zombie Attack are a bit like 'sims'. They place you in a situation where you must react to your environment and take on a challenging role. To become good at these games, choose a simulator you have a strong interest in.

Simulators can have many on-screen details, leaderboards and readings to keep an eye on. Mobile phones are frequently part of gameplay, and they provide **feedback and details** on your achievements. You can experiment to see if your score is **boosted** by doing a particular action. The chat window may also be used by gamers to reveal a top tip.

If you can **totally boss** a racing car, for example, get behind the wheel of a vehicle sim and floor it! If you haven't had much simulator game time, **ignore the various challenges at first** and just practise getting used to the game and its controls. Even if you constantly die, your effort perfecting things such as functions, vehicles and basic movements will be **invaluable** later on. Search for in-game vids and any captions that advise you what to do.

DIVE ON IN!

TAKE THE PLUNGE
<----------- AND TRY A SIMULATOR
GAME!

MINING SIMULATOR

Fans of Minecraft are often drawn to Mining Simulator. On one level it's a cool mining game based around materials, ores and coins, but 'dig' deeper and for pros it becomes a **heavily tactical game**! Find and enter codes to progress, target valuable minerals and pick up hats to increase powers. If you're flush with Robux, get the **Infinite Backpack** to speed things up.

SIMULATOR: EXPERT APPEAL

- ☑ Choose quick or longer games
- ☑ First-person fun
- ☑ Master new skills
- ☑ Escape to different worlds

STATS

👍 **VISITS** 491 million

🔧 **DATE CREATED** February 2018

👤 **CREATED BY** Rumble Studios

👥 **MAX PLAYERS** 10

DINOSAUR SIMULATOR

Want to know what it would have been like to be a dinosaur? This game might well be the closest chance you've got! You can raise your own young but just be sure to **watch out for deadly predators**. Word of advice – get smart and make friends quickly because being part of a herd can give you a way better chance of survival – safety in numbers and all that!

STATS

👍 **VISITS** 141 million

🔧 **DATE CREATED** March 2015

👤 **CREATED BY** ChickenEngineer

🎮 **MAX PLAYERS** 20

VEHICLE SIMULATOR

One of the best racing games ever uploaded to ROBLOX! Use it as an action game where **good guys and bad guys collide**, or if you're a pure petrol head, just race and roar on the roads. A highway race is only for the brave and experienced drivers. Target a **sleek speedster**, like a Lambo, Pagani or Nissan Skyline, with plenty of grip and drift to last the long course. Drift King races are also for advanced drivers.

STATS

👍 **VISITS** 354 million

🔧 **DATE CREATED** August 2014

👤 **CREATED BY** Simbuilder

🎮 **MAX PLAYERS** 18

MCLAREN 650S GT3

PET SIMULATOR

With more than 500 million visits within a year of its release, Pet Simulator is already **up there with the best sim experiences**. Made by BIG Games Simulators, you search for coins, eggs and chests in biomes and trade and upgrade your pet. For PC and Mac, use the 'I' and 'O' buttons to zoom in and out of your character and pet's view. If you're further away, you'll see more of what's happening around you.

STATS

👍 **VISITS** 541 million

🔧 **DATE CREATED** April 2018

👤 **CREATED BY** BIG Games Simulators

🧍 **MAX PLAYERS** 10

LUMBER TYCOON 2

It has 'Tycoon' in the title, but it's still a simulator experience! Playing Lumber Tycoon shows you that **not all sim games are stressful and ultra-competitive**. Chopping and trading wood is very relaxing. Aim for higher-value wood, like birch wood, and target a Sawmax machine to max out your money-raising capabilities.

⭐ EXPERT BONUS!

Pairing up with friends in simulator games can be rewarding. Farming trees in a small team will really boost your cash flow.

STATS

👍 **VISITS** 509 million

🔧 **DATE CREATED** July 2009

👤 **CREATED BY** Defaultio

🧍 **MAX PLAYERS** 6

SURVIVAL GAMES

SURVIVAL GAMES MAY SEEM LIKE AN EASY GENRE TO EXPLAIN BUT THEY'RE ACTUALLY PRETTY TRICKY. SO HERE GOES...

Clearly the aim is to survive and reach new levels or status – this type of scenario also exists in game types like First Person Shooter, Action, Simulator and Super Hero. For an adrenaline rush and buzz, few games can beat a blast of survival!

Disaster Warning:

Volcanic Eruption! Get away from the volcano

EXPERT BONUS!

Learn to 'read' the environment and landscape. In Natural Disaster Survival, looking up at the skies will reveal what weather type is coming!

How much health or power your avatar has is usually the **key to staying in the game**. After starting with maximum levels, players will be knocked back after stuff like contact with enemies or exposure to weather. Look for bonuses, shields or boosts that either automatically restore health or can be used when your levels drop.

Max your survival powers by levelling up with items that will give you a **major lifeline**. In the Zombie Attack game, invincibility and super speed are the two hottest extras to pick up. There's a good chance that they'll appear in the same spot the next time you play.

Survival games can involve weapons or tools, with **force needed against NPC enemies** or other gamers on the server. Instead of always being the hero, it's **best to avoid conflict** if you can and preserve your health by being stealthy and silent!

BLAST OFF!

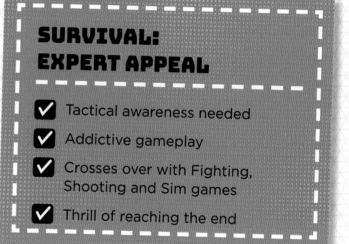

SURVIVAL: EXPERT APPEAL

- ☑ Tactical awareness needed
- ☑ Addictive gameplay
- ☑ Crosses over with Fighting, Shooting and Sim games
- ☑ Thrill of reaching the end

NATURAL DISASTER SURVIVAL

BATTLE AGAINST THE ELEMENTS AND TACKLE ANY EPIC HAZARD THAT COMES YOUR WAY. NATURAL DISASTER SURVIVAL IS THE ULTIMATE SURVIVAL GAME!

WILD WEATHER

From the lobby you are teleported into one of 16 maps. Just before the disaster strikes, you'll need to use the Disaster Warning system to **pre-plan your next move**. Sometimes the approaching disaster can be predicted by looking at the weather patterns around you. Clouds could mean thunder, tornado or blizzard. Sunny weather may signal wildfires or a volcanic eruption.

WHAT IS IT?

There are 11 disasters in total, including tornado, flood, thunderstorm, fire, blizzard, acid rain and volcano. The more you play and practise, the more escape tactics you'll master and the longer you'll stay in the game!

EXPERT BONUS!

Watch out for double and even triple disaster events. An earthquake and tsunami together could spell the end of your survival hopes!

STATS

👍 **VISITS** 840 million

🔧 **DATE CREATED** March 2008

👤 **CREATED BY** Stickmasterluke

👥 **MAX PLAYERS** 30

SHELTER

It's generally a **good tactic** to take shelter away from the open and inside buildings. You'll then have more cover from thunderous and windy conditions, but in high-rising floods you will become trapped. It is possible to **escape a twisty tornado** by running on the edge of the map, although this is a high-risk strategy.

HEDGE YOUR BETS

Don't assume that landing on or climbing to the highest point of buildings is the best option. If earthquakes make the building unstable, you'll suffer fall damage that could be **critical**. Climb to midway and then decide to go up or down when the disaster unfolds.

FIRST-PERSON SHOOTERS

HUNT DOWN TARGETS AND ENEMIES, COMPLETE MISSIONS, SET HIGH SCORES AND DODGE DANGER AS YOU FOCUS ON BECOMING A 'SHOOTING STAR!'

Take aim and get involved. The nature of FPSs means that you see the screen just as your avatar does. You get a great view, but some expert gamers still prefer a third person angle and will zoom out and change the perspective.

FPS: EXPERT APPEAL

- ✓ Packed with adventure
- ✓ Real-world feel
- ✓ Tactical and frantic
- ✓ Epic console-like graphics

Use a target sighting option if the FPS game has one to improve **aim and accuracy**. This is also known as aim down sights (ADS). Take every option you can to upgrade weapons and improve your arsenal. Team-work can be vital in FPS games. The Call of ROBLOX game requires teaming up in squads to take down NPC enemies and collect rewards for **wiping out waves of attacks**. Keep communication channels open with your team.

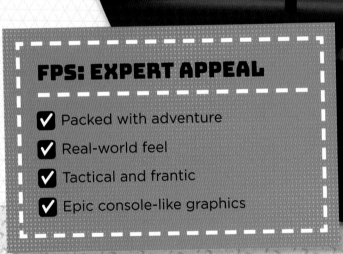

AIM AND FIRE! - - - - →

PHANTOM FORCES

Phantom Forces is the boss of FPS games! With over 700 million visits and thousands of users online at the same time, it's a **frantic shoot 'em up** based on advanced tactics and sharp squad play as the rival phantom and ghost teams do battle.

The team with the most kills in a timed shootout wins, so it's crucial to know what to have as your primary and secondary weapons. If you're a **pro shot** from a distance, take a sniper rifle but don't use the laser guide as this may alter your accuracy. Balance the sniper with a quick-fire backup (secondary) weapon, like a light machine gun.

STATS

👍 **VISITS** 719 million

🔧 **DATE CREATED** August 2015

👤 **CREATED BY** StyLiS Studios

🧱 **MAX PLAYERS** 32

ADVENTURE GAMES

DON'T GO THINKING THAT THE ADVENTURE GENRE IS JUST FOR ROBLOX NEWBIES – THESE GAMES CAN REQUIRE COMPLEX GAME STRATEGIES AND PLENTY OF PRACTICE!

Many of these games involve you becoming a hero and completing quests against the clock or enemies. It might just be a leaderboard-based adventure, or a simple hide and seek challenge. If you have spare Robux, spend a few coins on player upgrades and items.

ADVENTURE GAMES: EXPERT APPEAL

- ☑ Full of quests
- ☑ Amazing environments
- ☑ Combine action and strategy
- ☑ Become the hero

APOCALYPSE RISING

It's **all about defeating zombies** in this awesome adventure game. Be aware that unless you sprint, the creepy creatures in Apocalypse Rising are **faster than you**. And military zombies are much more dangerous than normal ones. Use a primary weapon like an AK-47, with a large magazine size that doesn't need constant reloading.

Sprinting seems like the best way to escape zombie waves, although it will quickly reduce your Thirst and Hunger. Monitor these levels at the bottom of your screen and use speed bursts carefully.

STATS

👍 **VISITS** 200.9 million

🔧 **DATE CREATED** April 2008

👤 **CREATED BY** Gusmanak

🏃 **MAX PLAYERS** 10

HIDE AND SEEK EXTREME

One of the simplest adventure games, but also **one of the most addictive!** Watch out for the 'IT' seeker using special tools, like glue, cameras and sprint, to hunt you down. Use bounce pads to reach high spots and hold your nerve – sometimes running away when IT is close is a bad move!

STATS

👍 **VISITS** 640 million

🔧 **DATE CREATED** January 2015

👤 **CREATED BY** Tim7775

🏃 **MAX PLAYERS** 14

⭐ EXPERT BONUS!

When you're hiding and IT is out of sight, keep your ears tuned for the sound of nearby footsteps – it's a sure sign you're about to be spotted.

BUILDING GAMES

CHOOSE YOUR MATERIALS WISELY

BUILDING IS A BIG FACTOR IN THIS ONLINE GAMING UNIVERSE.

From simple structures to complex settings and scenes, games like Build Battle, Sandbox, Building Simulator and Theme Park Tycoon challenge your building abilities. It's time to put down some strong foundations for your own construction empire!

EXPERT BONUS!

Remember that to use ROBLOX Studio you'll need to be on a PC or Mac. Xbox and Switch users can still play games created by Studio, though.

STUDIO SET-UP

ROBLOX Studio is the place to build your own games. It can be downloaded and used just like the normal ROBLOX game. Pros will have spent **hours and hours** getting used to the functions and abilities, but even for a newb, within 30 minutes you can construct a basic building! Look through toolbox for lists of pre-made features to drop into your world and the terrain editor lets you quickly place scenes like mountains and grassland.

BUILDING: EXPERT APPEAL

- ☑ Lots of updates and rewards
- ☑ Builds on Studio knowledge
- ☑ Develops essential skills
- ☑ Drives your imagination

BUILDING SIMULATOR

Released in March 2019 and racking up 15 million visits in just two months, Building Simulator has become a **smash hit**. Developed by Just For Fun, the plan is to make builds selected from blueprints, raise cash and then create more advanced builds for more cash. Simple, but fun!

The rebirthing function is key – it turns blueprints into gold, triples their value and pockets you more money. **Make rebirthing a priority**. Use the cash leaderboard, in the top right of the screen, to spur you on to bag more rewards. And the 'idle update' allows players to build huge buildings even when they're offline. Get the NPC helpers to assist on bigger builds, **freeing you up** for other tasks. The Golden Time Machine, at 4,999 Robux, gives you the most monstrous building skills.

★ EXPERT BONUS!

'Sandbox' describes games where players explore and edit. Sandbox 1 and 2 are also cool building titles, made by NullSenseStudio, for construction fans.

STATS

👍 **VISITS** 18.9 million

🔧 **DATE CREATED** March 2019

👤 **CREATED BY** Just For Fun™

🧱 **MAX PLAYERS** 7

OBSTACLE GAMES

SLOW OR FAST, COMPLEX OR BASIC, FUTURISTIC OR ORDINARY – OBSTACLE PLATFORM GAMES OFFER SOMETHING FOR EVERY ROBLOX FAN!

They are equally great for a quick five-minute blast or a tense two-hour session. Just save your progress and return each time to continue the quest.

It's a good idea to **jot down any shortcuts, tips or secrets** you discover on a piece of paper so that you remember them for the next time. The objective is usually to get from A to B, finish a level and move on.

Try to reach spawn points in an obstacle course. That way you know that if you're unlucky to die or be wiped out, as least you'll respawn in a checkpoint location you've already crossed. Returning to the beginning is a **nightmare!**

⭐ EXPERT BONUS!

These titles are simply known as 'obby' games in the ROBLOX world. Saying 'obstacle courses' with your mates is deffo not cool, bro!

OBSTACLES: EXPERT APPEAL

- ☑ Set records and reach levels
- ☑ Team or solo games
- ☑ Discover hidden features
- ☑ Build your own in Studio

For an obstacle course with **more of a story and a twist**, try games like Escape From The Prison, and Escape The School obby. In some of these games you can use Robux to skip levels, which is a super-sneaky shortcut! Keep a close-up view of your character because this will help you coordinate your jump moves easier over the obstacles.

Stay away from red-hot lava squares and bricks because these will **eliminate you instantly**. Teleport areas are a real game changer – enter into one and you'll be **zapped** to a new zone. Speed-boost tiles are also pretty special and put a spring in your step!

If there are other users in the game, sometimes **hanging back** and seeing how they tackle and navigate a section of the obby is very helpful. Learn from other people's experience and mistakes!

SPORTS GAMES

TRACKSUITS, TRAINERS AND DRINKS BOTTLES AT THE READY – IT'S TIME FOR A SPORTY SELECTION OF ROBLOX ADVENTURES!

There are hundreds of sport-based titles to choose, offering skills challenges and technical tests on heaps of activities.

⭐ EXPERT BONUS!

Look out for official ROBLOX Sports events. The first was in 2017 and players needed three prizes in three games to win cool virtual gear.

Why not try a game of Dodgeball? You'll join the red or the blue team and the aim is to throw balls at your opponents. Inflict four hits on a player and they are eliminated. Or maybe NBA Phenom? Get on the court and **slam dunk** your way to a sporting victory! In a third-person setup, **aim just a little higher** than the shot clock to loop the ball in the basket.

SPORTS: EXPERT APPEAL

- ☑ Level up to boost gameplay
- ☑ Lifelike action
- ☑ All major sports covered
- ☑ Mixes obby, tycoon and sim games

KICK OFF

This simple soccer game is one of the **coolest sports games** out there. Credits are earned by scoring goals, making passes and winning games in five-versus-five match-ups. Use hotkeys (E, R and T on PC) to shout commands to your team. Scope out the level of the team-mates you're paired with by **checking their career goals** and passes stats in the scoreboard, which is in the top right of your screen.

Zoom out for a wide-angle shot of the pitch, so you can see the whole game in action and where players are positioned. Using your controls, **master the power, sprint and trick shot commands**. A trick shot of spinning past the goalie and opposition defenders can see you breeze through on goal to score.

ROBOWLING

This test of your ten-pin bowling is one of the **most fun sports games**. The aiming line and cursor are there to guide your ball towards the pins, but don't always max out the power meter. A gentle bowl can be needed if you want to pick up a spare with your second ball. Switch to the 'ball cam' view for a close-up as you strike the pins. Remember that you have a 30-second limit between bowls!

👍 **VISITS** 132 million

🔧 **DATE CREATED** November 2015

👤 **CREATED BY** CM Games

🧍 **MAX PLAYERS** 8

STATS

👍 **VISITS** 9.1 million

🔧 **DATE CREATED** January 2016

👤 **CREATED BY** RoBowling

🧍 **MAX PLAYERS** 20

STATS

SUPER HERO GAMES

NOT ALL SUPER HEROES WEAR CAPES AND MASKS... SOME ACCESSORISE WITH A KEYBOARD OR A GAME PAD!

This genre often has big budgets and talented developers. You don't need to be a fan of Superman or Spiderman to love these games... but it helps!

The best place to start could be Super Hero Life III. The detail in this powerful game is awesome. Top-level gamers **spend an age** in the SHL lobby, choosing characteristics, powers, properties, dimensions, suits and designs. For the **true comic-book feel**, write a backstory for your avatar.

SUPER HERO: EXPERT APPEAL

- ☑ Fighting, survival & RPG
- ☑ Marvel and DC characters
- ☑ Expansive environments
- ☑ Fine tune your avatar's details

SUPER HERO TYCOON

Developed by Super Studios, a cool group of ROBLOX creators, there are several official Super Hero Tycoon games to pick from and power up. The basic principle is to **build an epic super hero base** by earning lots of cash. Rack up the money by building droppers, which load up cubes onto a conveyor and bring big bucks to your bank balance. Get codes to help you collect in-game items and tall 'mega droppers' for extra cash. Try taking on other heroes and **testing your special abilities**.

STATS

👍 **VISITS** 863 million

🔧 **DATE CREATED** December 2016

👤 **CREATED BY** Super Heroes™

👥 **MAX PLAYERS** 10

IRON MAN SIMULATOR

As Tony Stark, aka Iron Man, you're on a mission to collect and upgrade your super suits to get **extra abilities** and be able to battle other gamers. Each 'mark' of suit has a different health and power status and your health is reduced from enemy attacks. Keep the sound turned on with this game – the noise when you get **suited up and fire your repulsors** is incredible!

STATS

👍 **VISITS** 41 million

🔧 **DATE CREATED** May 2018

👤 **CREATED BY** Serphos

👥 **MAX PLAYERS** 15

PUZZLE GAMES

THERE'S A WHOLE GENRE OF BRAIN-BUSTING, HEAD-SCRATCHING AND CHIN-STROKING GAMES THAT WILL KEEP YOU PUZZLED FOR HOURS!

Either in single or multiplayer mode, puzzle games offer so much entertainment and intrigue. For lots of advanced ROBLOX users they are a welcome break from RPG or Tycoon-focused titles. Many of them can have education and teaching-based themes, but don't go thinking that puzzles are boring – jump in for a taste of the quiz action!

★ EXPERT BONUS!

Don't be too bigheaded and refuse to play the tutorial in a puzzle game! If offered, these helpful guides and walkthroughs usually give lots of clues and tips.

CAN YOU CRACK IT?

PUZZLES: EXPERT APPEAL

- ☑ Solo or team play
- ☑ Thought provoking
- ☑ Maths and common-sense tests
- ☑ Race against the clock

ESCAPE ROOM

Escape Room has attracted over 50 million visits since 2017. This tough test requires thought, sharp vision and the ability to question everything. It's a simple idea; all you have to do is escape the room by investigating what's around you, crack a code or puzzle and use it to escape through the door. **Click on objects** that may look strange, look high as well as low, use tools and props... and **never give up**!

DISCOVER

There are more than 20 rooms and maps to encounter. In single-player these include the prison, bank, jungle, school, treasure cave and wood cabin. Multiplayer options are the theatre, Pharaoh temple, lava lab and others. **Games are against the clock**, which brings extra pressure as the minutes tick by.. Note down any codes or clues on a piece of paper and watch out for things written on walls and signs. Remember, there's no pause option in Escape Room – it's all in real time!

AND THE WINNER IS...

Escape Room is so famous it has won two Bloxy awards. These are official ROBLOX prizes handed out every year. In 2018, Escape Room was voted **Best Single Player game** and the previous year it collected the Hardest Game gong. Good work, dudes!

STATS

👍 **VISITS** 53 million

🔧 **DATE CREATED** March 2017

👤 **CREATED BY** DevUltra

👣 **MAX PLAYERS** 20

MINI GAMES

THE MINIGAME GENRE IS A WHOLE BUNCH OF SMALL GAMES WITHIN ONE BIG GAME.

Complete one game, move on, finish another, collect points or coins and reach new levels. Pretty sweet, huh? Often the games are completely different, so the advanced ROBLOX users have to be multi-skilled and able to switch focus swiftly from using one ability to another.

MINIGAMES: EXPERT APPEAL

- ✔ Mix of player abilities
- ✔ Easy to understand
- ✔ Fast paced
- ✔ Wide range of skills needed

EPIC MINI GAMES

This remains the ultimate title to take on a **stack of unique and cool adventures** in the same session. By 2019 there were 87 different games to reach and master, including new additions like Ring Diver, Mower Mania and Romper Stomper.

GET ENTERING

Complete missions and daily quests to improve your cosmetics. Epic Minigames often links up for official ROBLOX Events such as Kids' Choice Awards, Egg Hunt and ROBLOX Holiday. Enter these events to work out how accomplished you are against others, and also **scoop exclusive items** like hats, suits and badges.

BADGES OF HONOUR

Reward badges are the perfect way to show off your **Epic Minigames mastery**! With around 40 available, you'll want to pick up Expert, Pro, Legend, Myth, Demigod and Epic as soon as you can. You'll need to accomplish levels 20 to 40 first, though.

HAT HUNT

You need to be in the lobby area in order to be transported to the next game. Before the action begins, explore the building and search for five special hats. Once found, the door to the **secret mine** can be opened and you'll receive an epic gift for your efforts!

BE READY

Most games last between 60 to 90 seconds, so you must **get up to speed super quickly**! If you're new to the game, follow what other gamers in the room are doing. Know what the basic control and function buttons are – be ready to shoot, jump, strike, step through, launch, push, freeze, collect... the missions are so varied!

STATS

👍 **VISITS** 683 million

🔧 **DATE CREATED** July 2015

👤 **CREATED BY** TypicalType

🧍 **MAX PLAYERS** 12

BATTLE ROYALE GAMES

FIGHTING GAMES CROSS INTO GENRES LIKE SURVIVAL, TOWN AND CITY AND FIRST-PERSON SHOOTER, BUT THERE ARE MANY OTHER UNIQUE STYLES AND FEATURES FOR ROBLOX COMBAT.

Stay calm, folks, and take the fight to the enemy! In recent years the Battle Royale genre of fighting and adventure games has exploded. Helped by the success of the videogame Fortnite, these games see solo or squad players drop into an area and fight to be the last one standing.

In titles such as Alone Battle Royale and Deadlocked, when you land make sure you get equipped with an effective mid-range weapon, like a shotgun, and **go on the attack straight away**. Keep communicating with your squad and look to take high spots. It's easier to spy on and target other players from a higher position!

⭐ EXPERT BONUS!

These games can include elements like mystery and comedy, but they're all linked by hand-to-hand combat or using weapons.

Health and Armor status is vital. Keep checking the map, often placed in the top right, to work out your location. When you're told that the storm is moving, for example, pay attention and work out your next move!

In solos, if you can find a quiet area of a map or location away from others, it can be a good time to practise your aiming and shooting at objects. **Get to know the crucial keys and buttons** to press, especially how to fire your weapon and run quickly for cover.

Expert fighters who play in busy games often like to check on the Performance Stats of their PC, Mac or console. In 'settings', click on the Performance Stats option and a detailed bar will appear across the top of the screen. Here you can **monitor things** like internet speed and the amount of memory you have.

EXPERT BONUS!

In busy battle royale games where the servers are packed, decreasing the graphics quality (in 'settings') can help improve problems with lag.

Choosing to team up with others means you need to work as a unit and **stick close together**. When you fall from your plane or helicopter, keep scanning the skies to see where others are heading to. Deploying your parachute early means your drop to the ground will take longer and you could suffer enemy fire.

BATTLE ROYALE: EXPERT APPEAL

- ✔ Melee and weapon combat
- ✔ Thrilling adventures
- ✔ Single or multiplayer options
- ✔ New games and updates

GET IN ----➔
THE ZONE

QUICK QUIZ: ROBLOX REWIND!

SHOW US THAT YOU'RE A PRO ROBLOX GAMER BY ANSWERING THIS SPEEDY SELECTION OF QUESTIONS. ALL THE CLUES CAN BE FOUND IN THIS GUIDE BOOK!

1

WHAT DO THE INITIALS 'VR' MEAN?

A.   Vehicle ROBLOX

B.   Very Recommended

C.   Virtual Reality

2

IF YOU'RE SOMEONE WHO BUILDS ROBLOX GAMES, WHAT ARE YOU KNOWN AS?

A.   A Constructor

B.   A Developer

C.   A Smarty-pants

3

WHICH OF THESE IS NOT A GENUINE ROBLOX GAME GENRE?

A.   All Genres

B.   Comedy

C.   Dance

4

WHAT IS THE GUI?

A.   Graphical User Interface

B.   Generate User Interaction

C.   Gather Ultimate Information

5

FROM THIS LIST, WHICH GAME HASN'T REACHED 2 BILLION VISITS?

A.   Phantom Forces

B.   MeepCity

C.   Jailbreak

6

WHAT ARE THE OFFICIAL ROBLOX AWARDS CALLED?

A.   Screen Stars

B.   Bloxys

C.   Avatar Awards

7

WHEN DISCUSSING WHICH WEAPONS TO USE FIRST AND SECOND, WHAT IS THIS USUALLY CALLED?

A.   Weapon switching

B.   Gun getting

C.   Primary and secondary fire

8

WHICH OF THESE TERMS IS NOT USED WHEN DECIDING HOW TO WIN A GAME?

A.   Glitching

B.   Strategy

C.   Tactics

9

IN WHICH YEAR DID ROBLOX LAUNCH THE RTHRO SYSTEM FOR AVATARS?

A.   2006

B.   2011

C.   2018

10

WHAT DOES THE ROBLOX TERM NPC MEAN?

A.   Not Properly Controlled

B.   Non-playable Characters

C.   Non-playable Computers

PRO PLAYER POWER

ROBLOX GAMING GLOSSARY

ARTIFICIAL INTELLIGENCE

Commonly called AI, it describes interactions and behaviour in games from things like characters, environments and vehicles.

AFK

In chat mode or when you're communicating with friends, the phrase AFK means you are currently Away From Keyboard.

BADGES

Whether you're a ROBLOX pro or a beginner, it's always epic to earn in-game badges for achievements like reaching levels and completing quests!

BOT

A nickname for a robotic character. Sometimes it's a cheeky phrase to describe a new, or 'newbie', ROBLOX gamer still getting used to the game!

CAMERA ANGLES

In many games you can change the position you are viewing the action from. Some games have first person camera angle, which means you see the action through the eyes of your avatar. Third person angle means you can see your avatar running around.

CUSTOMIZE

If you customize in ROBLOX it means you edit or change something. For example, this can be something specific in gameplay or the simple appearance of your avatar.

GAME PASSES

In-game extras that can give you access to secret locations, new powers or items. Usually these must be bought with Robux.

GG

An increasingly popular term in all computer games. It means 'good game' and is a compliment and friendly term used between players.

GLITCH

An error or fault in ROBLOX can be called a glitch. Sometimes glitches can be fun to experience, but they are often quickly fixed by developers.

HOTKEYS

These are the buttons or controls you use most of the time in a game, either across PC, Mac or consoles. Hotkeys can be changed to suit a player's style.

ICON

From the ROBLOX games page, all games are represented by a picture icon. It sums up what the game is about and how many people are playing.

LAG

Visual delays in games, when characters appear to suffer from being out of sync with the action, is often referred to as lagging.

LOBBY

At the beginning of many ROBLOX games, players have to wait in an area called the lobby. In the lobby, player servers and assets can be loaded.

MELEE

When a ROBLOX avatar is battling an opponent close-up, this is known as melee fighting. It is similar to close-quarters combat (CQC).

PVE

Player versus Environment. In games where your avatar comes up against monsters, armies or baddies, you're in the fascinating world of a PvE adventure!

PVP

PvP stands for Player versus Player. It can describe a solo game when individuals compete against each other, or a solo match-up in a team game.

SPAWN

This means the creation, rebirth or entering of a character or feature into a ROBLOX game. In obstacle games, players often respawn at a spawn point after dying.

TELEPORT

Players can be teleported into the beginning of a game or teleported to a different area. Teleporting is a fancy phrase for appearing without the physical motion of actually travelling!

UPDATE

ROBLOX developers are always keen to upgrade their games. It means they have been improved, changed and made better for users to enjoy.

PRO PLAYER POWER

ROBLOX DATA DETAILS

RECORD YOUR ROBLOX RECORDS, MISSIONS AND ACHIEVEMENTS HERE.

YEAR I JOINED ROBLOX:

MY AVATAR'S NAME:

MY AGE:

MY TOP 3 ROBLOX FRIENDS:

MY NO.1 ROBLOX GAME IS:

MY FAVOURITE ROBLOX DEVELOPER IS:

MY FAVOURITE ITEMS ARE:

MY ROBLOX DREAM IS TO:

I'M AN EXPERT IN THESE GAME GENRES:

☐ Role play
☐ Town and City
☐ Tycoon
☐ Survival
☐ Building
☐ Sports
☐ First Person Shooter
☐ Battle Royale
☐ Obstacle
☐ Simulator

IN THE FUTURE I'M GOING TO:

☐ Collect more Robux
☐ Become a developer
☐ Join the Builders Club
☐ Create fun ROBLOX content
☐ Win a Bloxy award